Project Editor Sue Grabham
Senior Contributing Editor Charlotte Evans
Assistant Editor Tara Benson
Section Editors Angela Holroyd, John Paton

Senior Designer Janice English
Staff Designers Sandra Begnor, Siân Williams
Section Designer Ch'en Ling
Additional Design Rachael Stone, Smiljka Surla

Publishing Director Jim Miles

Art Director Paul Wilkinson

Additional Art Preparation
Matthew Gore, Andy Archer, Shaun Deal,
Julian Ewart, Narinder Sahotay, Andy Stanford,
Janet Woronkowicz

Picture Research Elaine Willis
Artwork Archivist Wendy Allison
Artwork Researcher Robert Perry

Activity Artist Caroline Jayne Church

Indexer Hilary Bird

Production Manager Linda Edmonds
Production Assistant Stephen Lang

Contributing Authors Barbara Reseigh,
Dominique Rift, Brian Williams

Specialist Consultants
David Glover BSc, PhD (Science writer);
Professor B.W. Hodder BLit, MA, PhD
(School of Oriental and African Studies,
University of London);
Keith Lye BA, FRGS (Geography writer);
Julia Stanton BA DipEd (Australasia consultant)

Educational Consultants
Ellie Bowden (Curriculum Advisor for
Primary Science and Senior Teacher, Essex);
June Curtis (Primary School Teacher, Nottingham
and R.E. writer);
Kirsty Jack (Head Teacher, Primary
School, Edinburgh)

This edition published in 1995
by **The Southwestern Company UK Ltd**
by arrangement with Larousse plc

First published by Larousse plc 1994

A CIP catalogue record for this book is available from the British Library

ISBN 0 87197 429 0

Typeset by Tradespools Ltd, Frome, Somerset
Colour separation by P&W Graphics, Singapore
Printed in Italy

Kingfisher Learning Adventure Library

–5–
Science/People
and Places

SW
SOUTHWESTERN

Contents

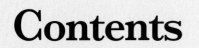

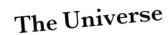

Activities

Before you start each activity, collect everything you need and make sure there is a clear space. Wash your hands before cooking and wear gloves when touching soil. Wear an apron for gluing, cooking and using paints.
If an adult is needed, ask if they can help before you start.
   Afterwards, make sure you clear up any mess and put everything away.

▷ Here are some of the materials that you might need for the activities. **Always** ask an adult before using anything that is not yours.

Recipe

500 g plain flour
150 g salt
1 mug water
food colouring

Make dough

Make dough for some of the modelling activities. Mix flour and salt in a bowl. If making coloured dough, add food colouring to water. Add as much water as needed to flour and salt, a little at a time. Stir. Turn out onto floured surface. Knead into a smooth dough. Make models. When finished, ask an adult to put them in the oven, on a low heat, for five hours. Paint the models when cool.

Science

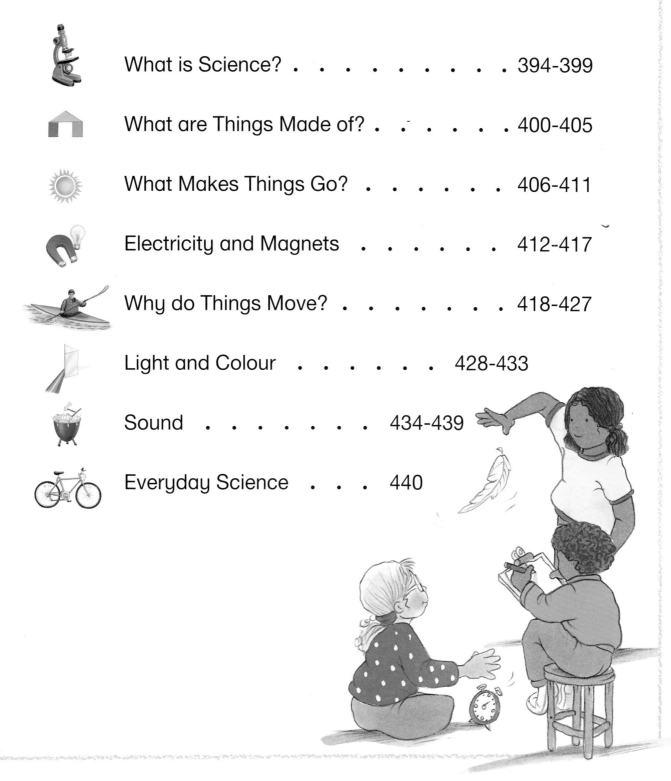

What is science?

Science is about finding out. It helps us make sense of our world. Science begins with observation. This means looking at things very carefully. Scientists work in different ways and study many subjects, such as biology, astronomy, medicine, geology and chemistry. Much has been discovered through science, but there is a lot left to find out about our world.

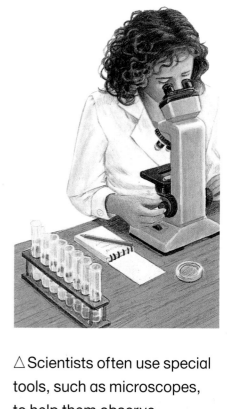

△ Scientists often use special tools, such as microscopes, to help them observe.

The senses
Observation does not mean using just our eyes, but all our senses to find out things.

touching a tree to see if it is smooth or rough

smelling an egg to see if it is bad

tasting a lemon to find out if it is sweet or sour

looking in a book to find answers to questions

listening for high and low sounds

△ We can all be scientists. These children are studying the wildlife in a pond.

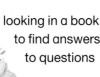
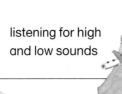

▷This scientist is a marine biologist. She is studying sea life.

△Astronomers use telescopes to study the stars. They find out about the Universe.

▽ Doctors study medicine. They do experiments, or tests, to find out if new drugs can fight diseases.

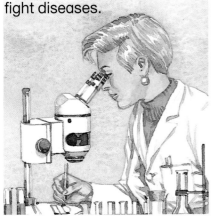

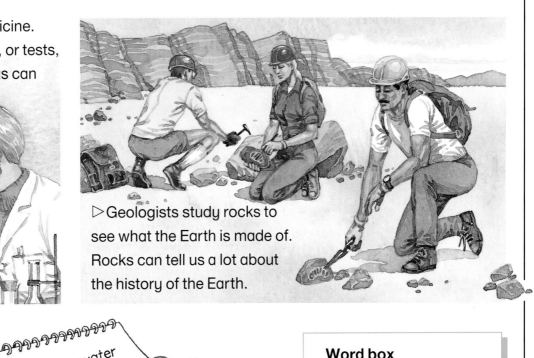

▷Geologists study rocks to see what the Earth is made of. Rocks can tell us a lot about the history of the Earth.

H_2O=water

▷Chemists use special symbols, or signs, to study chemistry. Doctors and other scientists use these symbols, too.

Word box
Observation is how we find out about the world around us. We need to use our senses to do this. **Experiments** are the tests scientists carry out to see if their ideas are correct.

How to be a scientist

Scientists see things happening and start to ask questions. Sometimes they guess at possible answers. Then they carry out experiments, or tests, to see if they were right. When scientists carry out experiments, they measure and record what is happening. They might do the same test several times. The results are often worked out with the help of computers.

△ We all ask questions. This boy is asking how heavy planes manage to stay up in the sky.

◁ His sister is trying to find out about planes by looking up the information in a book.

graph

▷ Computers may be used by scientists to record and make sense of information. This scientist is using a computer to make a graph with the results of his experiment.

△ An exciting way of finding out answers is to test things for yourself. The question on the clipboard is to be tested.

△ Equal amounts of dry soil are put into two trays. The same number of seeds are sown in each tray. The trays are placed side by side.

Can you stop an apple from turning brown?

You can be a scientist too! Try this experiment. Ask an adult to cut an apple into four pieces. Put each piece onto a plate. Place one piece in the fridge. Wrap the second piece in foil and sprinkle lemon juice on the third. Leave the fourth alone. Do they all go brown?

△ Every day the right-hand tray is watered. The left-hand tray is not watered at all.

△ The watered tray has seedlings growing. The other tray has none. The test has shown that seeds will not grow without water.

Time

Time is very important to scientists. They often need to measure exactly how long it takes something to happen.

Over thousands of years, people have invented different clocks. Candles, shadows and sand have been used to measure the passing of hours and minutes. Today, scientists can measure in seconds and even tiny parts of a second, so their results can be extremely accurate.

shadow clock

digital alarm clock

sand clock

candle clock

stop clock

alarm clock

Clocks
These are all different kinds of clocks. Which ones have you used?

◁ These children are using a watch to time the number of drips in a minute.

▷ This boy has found out that the girl's skipping is slowing down as she gets tired.

Make a water clock

Ask an adult to make a hole in the bottom of a plastic pot. Tape on a string handle. Pin to an old table. Put another pot below. Pour water into top pot. After each minute, mark water level on bottom pot. Empty and refill to use as a minute clock.

Temperature

Thermometers are used to measure the temperature, or how hot, something is.

Scientists have to think about temperature when they are carrying out experiments. If two things are being compared, it is important that they are kept at the same temperature.

When scientists work in very hot or very cold places, they need to wear and use materials that are not damaged by these temperatures.

△ Different thermometers measure temperatures in different places. A wall thermometer measures the temperature of air in a room.

▽ Scientists in cold places, such as Antarctica, work in below-freezing temperatures. They have to wear special clothes to keep them warm.

△ Scientists that work near hot volcanoes must wear heat-resisting suits. This scientist is using a special thermometer that can measure high temperatures.

Materials and structures

The things around us are made from different materials, such as wood, plastic and metal. Different materials do different jobs. A sponge soaks up water. A metal saucepan is strong and can stand up to heat.

The way something is put together is called its structure. Structure can also help to make things strong.

△ These objects are made from many materials. Some are strong, some are soft and others stand up to heat.

△ This lighthouse is made from materials that can stand up to stormy weather.

△ The glass in a greenhouse lets the sun's rays pass through and traps heat, so the plants stay warm.

Word box
Materials are used to make things. Materials are carefully chosen to suit the jobs they have to do.
Structures are the ways materials are put together to make them stronger.

△ This bridge has stood for years. The stone it is made from is a strong material.

△ Skyscrapers are made from strong, hard materials that will last a long time.

Build a roof

Arrange two cereal packets alongside each other. These are your walls. Open a hardback book in the middle and try to balance it on the walls to make a roof. You will find that the weight of the roof pushes the two walls apart. Now lay two rulers across the cereal packets, as shown. Does the book balance now?

△ The shape of a structure is important. Cylinders look like tubes. They are very strong. A tree's cylinder-shaped trunk supports its heavy branches.

△ Stone columns on buildings are cylinder-shaped. They are able to hold up a lot of weight, such as roofs.

◁ Triangles are strong because no one side can bend away from the other two. The Eiffel Tower is made of many triangles.

▽ Spiders spin strong webs. Can you see the triangles in this web?

Solids, liquids and gases

All materials are either solids, liquids or gases. Solids keep their shape and can be hard or soft. Liquids take the shape of their container. If we pour a liquid, it will run. Gases will not even stay in their container. If they escape, they spread out all over the room.

△ Can you pick out the solids, gases and liquids in this picture?

Icarus
(A Greek myth)

Icarus and his father were imprisoned on the island of Crete. They escaped by making wings of feathers held together with wax. Icarus' father warned him not to fly too near the Sun. But Icarus ignored him. The Sun melted the wax, and Icarus fell.

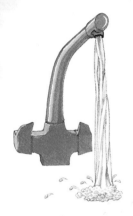

△ Some materials can turn from solid to liquid to gas. Water from a tap is liquid.

△ If we freeze water, it becomes a solid called ice. Ice melts back into water.

△ If we heat water enough, it becomes a gas called steam. This change is called boiling.

△ If we let steam cool, it turns back into a liquid. This change is called condensation.

▷ Many materials change when they are heated or cooled. Lava comes out of a volcano as a liquid. As lava cools, it turns into solid rock.

lava

△ As wax gets hot, it melts and goes runny. When it cools it becomes solid. Wax can change again and again.

◁ Some things change when they are heated, but cannot change back. A fried egg cannot go back to being raw.

▽ Milk left for a long time goes lumpy and smelly. You cannot undo this change.

Make an ice pop freezer
Put about 20 ice cubes in a bowl. Push a liquid ice pop into bowl and cover with ice. Sprinkle a tablespoon of salt over ice so ice melts. A mixture of salt and ice is colder than ice on its own. After 15 minutes the ice pop will be solid.

▽ A baked cake cannot go back to being the runny mixture it was before it was cooked.

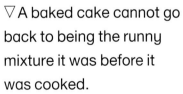

403

Mixing and dissolving

We often mix things together when we are cooking, but not everything mixes in the same way. Some things seem to disappear in water or other liquids. They have dissolved. Others soak up some of the liquid and go lumpy. Some do not mix at all, but float on top of liquids. Oil does not dissolve in water, it floats on the water's surface.

△ In cold water, salt dissolves quickly, sugar takes a longer time and flour goes lumpy.

How The Donkey Got Away
(A story by Jean de La Fontaine)

Two donkeys were being driven home from market. One carried heavy bags of salt, the other light sponges. The donkey carrying salt was forced to cross a stream. The salt dissolved in the water and the donkey escaped. The second donkey jumped in the stream, thinking he could escape too. But the sponges soaked up water and he had to be rescued from sinking.

△ Hot water helps things dissolve more easily, such as sugar in hot tea.

▽ We wash dirty plates in a mixture of water and detergent, or washing-up liquid. The detergent loosens the bits of food on the plates so they disperse in water more easily.

△ Cleaning gets rid of dirt by dispersing it. Mud from muddy boots disperses in water. This means that tiny bits of mud are in the water that is carried away down the drain.

▷ Large tankers carry tonnes of oil. Sometimes there is an accident and oil leaks. Here you can see an oil slick floating on top of the sea.

Evaporation

When something dissolves, it does not disappear. In the sun, the water in salty water evaporates, leaving the salt behind.

◁ Oil slicks affect all of our wildlife. This bird has been rescued and is being bathed in detergent to disperse the oil covering its feathers.

405

Energy

Energy is all around us. We cannot see it, but we can see, hear and feel its effects. When we watch the television, listen to the radio or feel a room warm up, energy is being used.

Energy does not disappear, it changes from one kind to another. Petrol has energy stored in it. When it is used in a car, petrol burns and gives out heat energy. As it makes the car go, the heat energy is turned into movement energy.

Make a windmill

Cut slits in a square of thin card, 24 cm by 24 cm. Make holes in middle and corners, as shown. Fold corners into middle and line up holes. Thread a pin through. Thread a bead on. Push pin through a strong plastic straw, a bead and a piece of cork. Blow windmill to spin it.

△ A sailing boat uses wind energy. This wind energy is caught in the boat's sails and pushes the boat forward.

◁ People and animals turn energy from the food they eat into movement energy.

△ Hairdryers work by turning electrical energy into heat and movement energy.

406

△ All living things get their energy from the sun.

△ Grass uses sunlight to make food. Cows eat the grass.

◁ Cows use energy from the grass to make milk.

◁ This energy helps us to lead an active life.

◁ We drink the milk, that contains energy.

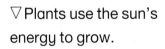

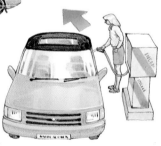

▽ Plants use the sun's energy to grow.

▷ Cars use the petrol to make them go.

◁ Today we drill for oil and turn it into other fuels, such as petrol.

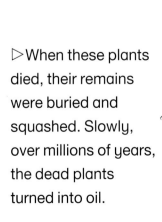

▷ When these plants died, their remains were buried and squashed. Slowly, over millions of years, the dead plants turned into oil.

Word box
Energy is the ability to do work. Everything needs energy to move, work, breathe or grow. **Fuel** is stored energy. It is burned to release heat energy to power machines.

Heat energy

When you hold a mug of hot cocoa, it warms your hands up. Holding a snowball makes your hands go very cold. This is because hot things pass their heat to their surroundings and lose some heat themselves. Heat always moves from a warmer place to a colder one. Heat energy moves through radiation, conduction or convection.

△ Conduction heats food in a pan. The heat from the cooker moves to the pan, and from the pan it moves to the food.

▽ The sun gives off rays of heat which warm up Earth. This is called radiation.

△ Heat from hot drinks warm up your hands by conduction.

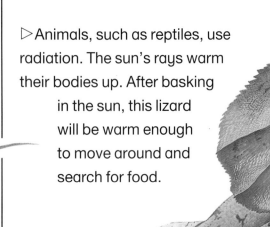

▷ Animals, such as reptiles, use radiation. The sun's rays warm their bodies up. After basking in the sun, this lizard will be warm enough to move around and search for food.

△ Heat from your hands is lost through conduction when you hold a snowball.

▽ This room is being heated by convection. Air near the radiator becomes warm. This warm air rises and is replaced by cooler air, which in turn is heated itself.

Conduction experiment
Some materials conduct heat better than others. To test this, put a wooden spoon, a plastic spoon and a metal spoon into a jug of warm water. Leave for two minutes. Feel the handles. The one that is the warmest conducts heat the best.

▷ Convection is important in heating homes. The warmest place is usually at the top because warm air rises.

▷ The middle of the house is warm, but not as warm as upstairs. The bottom of the house is coolest because cold air sinks. In old houses, the basement was often used as a store for keeping things cool.

Bigger and smaller

Most materials get bigger, or expand, when they get hotter. When materials get colder they usually get smaller, or contract. Solids, liquids and gases all expand and contract. It is important to know how materials will behave when we build different structures. The size of pipes, wires and buildings must allow for expansion and contraction.

△ Electric power cables contract in the winter, so they are almost straight.

△ In the summer heat, electric power cables expand and hang lower and looser.

△ Water is unusual. It expands as it freezes. This is why pipes can burst in winter.

△ Expanding ice in a water pipe cracks it. When the ice melts, water spurts out.

◁ Popcorn is made by expansion. Inside each grain of corn is a small amount of air.

▷ When the corn is heated, the air inside each grain expands.

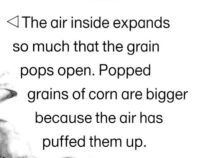

◁ The air inside expands so much that the grain pops open. Popped grains of corn are bigger because the air has puffed them up.

Expand water

Fill a plastic tub to the brim with water. Put the lid on. Ask an adult to put the tub in the freezer. As it freezes, the ice will expand and push the lid off the tub.

Saving energy

Most of the energy we use comes from fuels such as coal, gas or oil. But the Earth's supply of fuel will run out one day. Also, when we burn fuel to release its energy, we pollute, or poison, the air around us. So we must save energy when we can.

▽ Petrol for cars is made from oil. If we walked more, instead of driving, we could save oil.

▽ We can save energy so that fuels last longer and pollute less. We can switch off lights when they are not needed.

▽ Heating water takes up energy. A shower uses less hot water than a bath, so saves energy.

▽ Homes can be insulated to keep heat in. Gaps in between walls stop heat from being conducted through the bricks. The gaps are often filled with insulating materials. Double-glazed windows and loft insulation also stop warmth escaping.

▽ We can stop wasting heat by making sure that windows are closed when the heating is on.

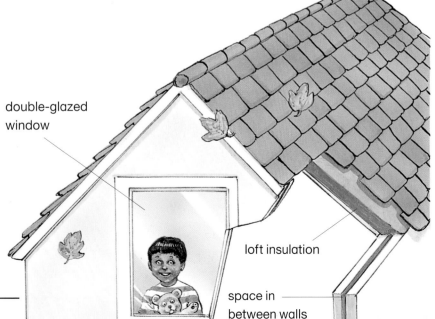

double-glazed window

loft insulation

space in between walls

Electricity

There are two types of electricity. They are static electricity and current electricity. Current electricity can flow along wires. This means that it can travel from a battery or a power station to where it is needed. Current electricity is very important in our everyday world. Just think of all the things that stop working if there is a power cut!

△ If you comb your hair quickly, it will become charged with static electricity.

Never play with, or go near, current electricity. It could kill you.

▷ These machines work by using current electricity. Without them, our lives would be very different, and much more difficult.

Word box
Power stations burn fuel to make current electricity for use at home and work.
Batteries make current electricity from chemicals stored inside them.

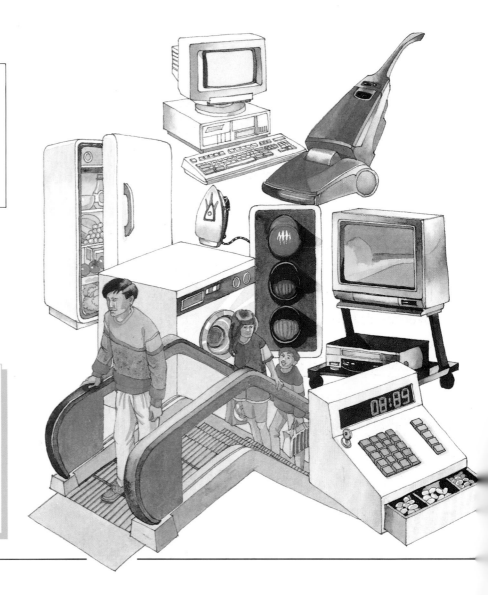

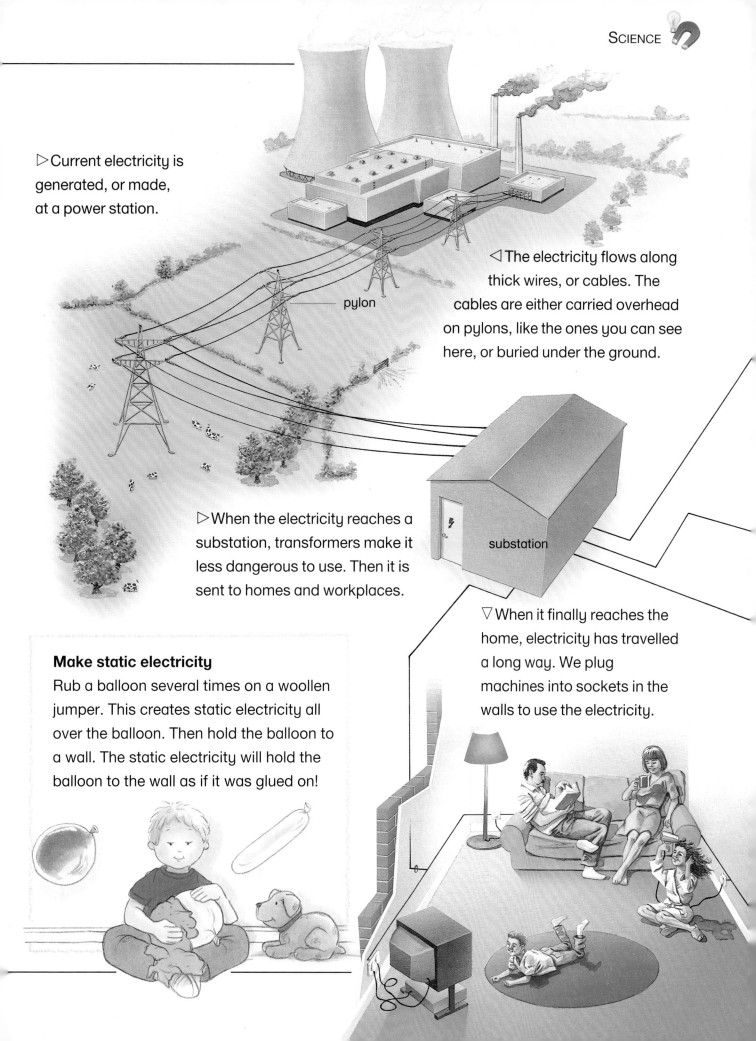

▷Current electricity is generated, or made, at a power station.

◁The electricity flows along thick wires, or cables. The cables are either carried overhead on pylons, like the ones you can see here, or buried under the ground.

pylon

▷When the electricity reaches a substation, transformers make it less dangerous to use. Then it is sent to homes and workplaces.

substation

▽When it finally reaches the home, electricity has travelled a long way. We plug machines into sockets in the walls to use the electricity.

Make static electricity

Rub a balloon several times on a woollen jumper. This creates static electricity all over the balloon. Then hold the balloon to a wall. The static electricity will hold the balloon to the wall as if it was glued on!

Batteries and circuits

Batteries make and store small amounts of electricity that can be carried anywhere. Chemicals inside a battery make the electricity. Some batteries can be recharged so they last longer. Others are finished once the chemicals have been used up.

Batteries are used in circuits. A circuit is a pathway that allows electricity to flow. As long as a circuit is complete, electricity will keep flowing.

△ Batteries are sold in many shapes and sizes. All these batteries use chemicals to make electricity. Once the chemicals are used up, the batteries stop working and should be thrown away.

▽ A car battery can be recharged. The battery stores electricity to start the car, and then is recharged when the engine is running.

Never take a battery apart. The chemicals inside are dangerous.

△ Batteries are used to power many things. Watches and calculators have tiny batteries. A much larger one is needed to run an electric wheelchair.

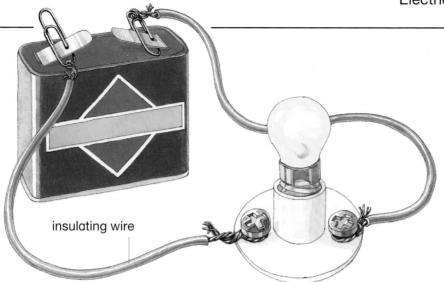

insulating wire

◁ This is a complete circuit. Electricity flows along a wire from one terminal, or end, of the battery. It passes through a light bulb and lights it up. Then it travels along the other wire, back to the other terminal of the battery.

▷ If there is a gap in a circuit, electricity cannot flow. This is how a switch works. It connects the circuit to turn things on and breaks the circuit to turn things off. Here, the switch is a paperclip. When both ends are no longer connected, it breaks the circuit and the light bulb goes out.

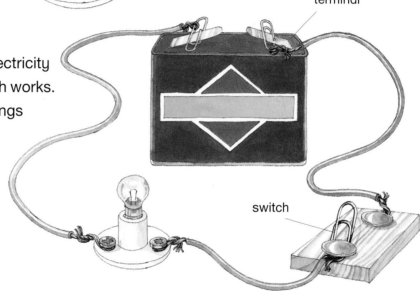

terminal

switch

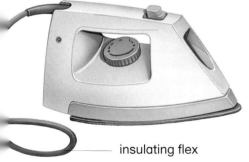

insulating flex

△ Electricity cannot flow through some materials. These are called insulators and make using electricity safer. The wires carrying electricity to this iron are covered by an insulating flex.

Make a simple circuit
Ask an adult to help with this activity. Screw a small bulb into a bulb holder. Strip 1 cm of insulating plastic from each end of two pieces of insulated wire. Attach to the bulb holder, as shown in pictures above. Attach a paperclip to the other ends. Clip them onto each terminal to light up the bulb.

415

Magnets

A magnet attracts, or pulls, some materials towards it. This is called magnetism and the materials are magnetic. Not everything is magnetic, so there are some things that you cannot pick up with a magnet.

Every magnet has a north pole and a south pole. These poles are at the ends of a magnet. The north pole of one magnet attracts the south pole of another magnet. Two north poles or two south poles repel, or push apart.

△ If you put the north pole of one magnet near the south pole of another, they are attracted and pull together.

▽ These materials are magnetic. When you put a magnet near them, they are attracted to it.

non-magnetic objects

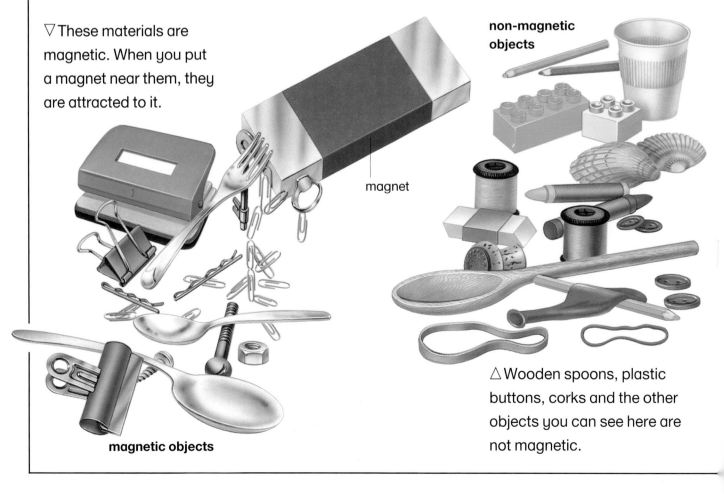

magnet

magnetic objects

△ Wooden spoons, plastic buttons, corks and the other objects you can see here are not magnetic.

▷Compasses are used to help people find their way. The needle in a compass is a magnet. As the Earth is magnetic, the north-seeking pole of the compass turns to the North Pole of the Earth.

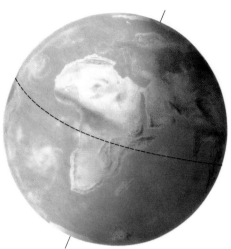

△The Earth itself is magnetic.

▷Magnets come in all sorts of shapes and sizes. This enormous magnet works in a breakers yard. The magnet picks up and moves huge pieces of scrap metal. It would be difficult to pick up this car without it!

Make a magnetic theatre

Cut slits in four short cardboard tubes. Splay out ends and glue to the bottom corners of a thin cardboard box. Decorate to look like a theatre. Add old material for curtains. Draw characters on thin card. Cut out, leaving a tab, as shown. Fold back tabs and tape on paperclips. Tape strong magnets to sticks. To move the characters, move one magnet under each character.

417

Backwards and forwards

Things move when something pushes or pulls them. These pushes and pulls are called forces. A force can make something start to move, speed up, slow down, change direction or stop moving. Every force has another force that pushes in the opposite direction.

△ All these children are using forces to make things move.

◁ Three children cannot make the see-saw work. This is because the force pushing down on one end is bigger than the force pushing down on the other end. So, one child is getting off.

Word box
Forces can make things move. Pushes and pulls are forces.
Pendulum is any weight that hangs from a fixed point and swings freely.

△ Two children make the see-saw work. The forces pushing on each end are the same.

Can you find?

1 push   4 pull

2 pull   5 push

3 push   6 pull

Make a pendulum

Tie a piece of string around a cotton reel. Attach the loose end of string to a soft block of wood, using a drawing pin, as shown. Fix the block of wood to the edge of an old table with plasticine. Push or pull your pendulum to make it swing. Use a stop clock to see how many swings it makes in 30 seconds. Try making the string longer and count the number of swings again. Are there more or less?

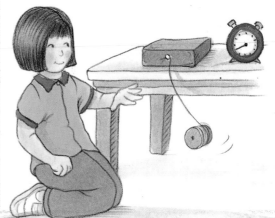

▷ When this canoeist pulls the paddle back, he pushes the canoe forwards.

Floating and sinking

An object floats on water because of balancing forces. As the weight of an object pulls it down, the water pushes it up. If an object is light for its size, the push of the water balances its weight and the object floats.

The shape of an object is also very important. It allows some heavy metal objects, such as ships, to float. This is because they push aside more water than they weigh themselves.

Find the answers

Do wooden spoons float?

What can we use to keep us afloat when swimming?

some objects float on top of the water's surface

some objects float almost completely under the water

some objects sink to the bottom

△ Some objects float on top of water, others sink to the bottom. Some float near the surface, just under the water.

420

Make a catamaran

A catamaran is a boat with two hulls. Ask an adult to cut a washing-up liquid bottle in half for hulls. Use waterproof tape to attach thin strips of balsa wood across the hulls, to hold them together.

Float your catamaran in water. How many objects can you put into your catamaran before it sinks?

▽ Air-filled armbands help you float. Air is lighter than water. Objects with lots of air trapped inside them float well.

△ A lump of plasticine sinks because it weighs more than the water pushing it up.

▽ The shape of a ship helps it float. This is because it has a lot of air inside it, so is light for its very large size. It pushes aside more water than it weighs itself.

△ If the plasticine is made into a boat, the water has a wider shape to push up. It floats because the plasticine is now lighter for its size.

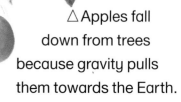

Gravity and weight

The Earth pulls everything towards its centre, including us! This force is called gravity. It is the reason why things always fall down and not up. The Earth's gravity pulls on the Moon too, which keeps it circling around the Earth.

The weight of an object depends on gravity. We call the pull of the Earth's gravity on an object its weight.

△ Apples fall down from trees because gravity pulls them towards the Earth.

▷ You can throw a ball up into the air, but it will always fall back to the ground.

◁ When scales measure your weight, they are measuring the pull of Earth's gravity on your body.

▷ In a spaceship far from the Earth, there is so little gravity that things just float around. Astronauts have to tie themselves down, if they do not want to float about.

Pressure

When you press your fist into clay, you make a dent. But if you use your finger, you make a deep hole. This is because of the different amounts of pressure, or forces, pushing on each area of clay. The weight of your fist is spread over a larger area than your finger, so there is less pressure and a shallower print.

▽ Your shoes make deep footprints in the snow.

▷ Tyres are full of air. The air's pressure keeps a truck moving along smoothly.

▽ Snowshoes make shallower footprints. Your weight is spread over a greater area, so there is less pressure.

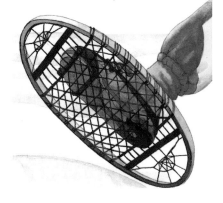

▽ You can see air pressure at work if you squeeze all the air from a plastic tube.

▽ When the tube's lid is taken off again, air pressure forces air back into the tube.

△ If the lid is put on while the tube is still squeezed, the tube will stay squeezed.

Stick or slip

Have you ever slipped on a wet floor? If so, it was because there was so little friction. Friction is the force that stops two surfaces from sliding past each other easily. There is little friction between slippery surfaces, and more friction between rough surfaces. The more friction there is between two surfaces, the hotter they become.

△ It is easy to slip with wet feet. People use bath mats because they increase friction.

◁ Special grips increase friction. With more friction, tyres and shoes are safer on slippery surfaces. Also, tennis rackets are less likely to slip out of a player's hand.

△ A smooth sledge slides easily over slippery snow.

▷ We put oil in a car's engine to reduce the friction between its moving parts. This helps the parts to move more easily and stops them getting too hot.

△ Squeaky doors need oil. The squeak is caused by friction in the metal hinges. Oil helps to reduce friction and stop the squeak.

The Wizard of Oz
(A story by L. Frank Baum)

When Dorothy found the Tin Man, he was stuck. She had to ease the friction in his joints with oil before he could move.

Have a friction race

Find objects that are made of different materials, but are about the same size. You could use an ice cube, a stone, a piece of sponge and a block of wood.

Rest thick, smooth card against some books to make a slope. Hold the objects at the top of the slope. Let them go at the same time. The first to the bottom has less friction than the rest.

△ You can feel the heat that friction makes when you rub your hands. Soapy hands have much less friction, so they do not warm up as much.

425

Moving through air

Moving through air slows things down. We call this air resistance. To make things move more quickly we make them a special shape. Many of them have smooth, rounded edges, which let air flow under, over and around them easily. These shapes are called streamlined.

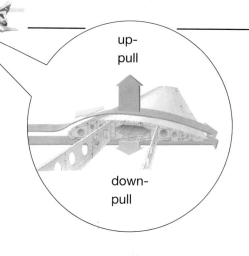

△ The streamlined wings of a plane help to keep it in the air. The up-pull of the air flowing over the wing balances the down-pull of its weight.

◁ Planes have a streamlined shape. This helps them to fly easily through the air.

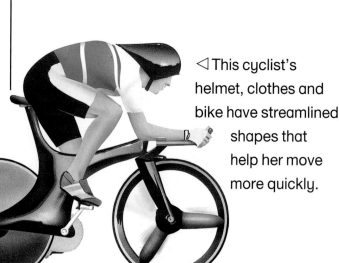

◁ This cyclist's helmet, clothes and bike have streamlined shapes that help her move more quickly.

△ The flying lemur does not actually fly. It has streamlined flaps of skin and a tail which help it to glide through the air.

426

Machines for moving

Simple machines can make moving things easier. Machines such as rollers and wheels help to reduce friction.

Levers are simple machines that help us lift heavy weights. A lever is a bar that swings on a fixed point, like a see-saw. Pushing one end of the lever down lifts a weight at the other end.

△ Stonehenge, England, was built 4,000 years ago. Its huge stones were probably pulled on rollers made of tree trunks.

▷These clowns are using a lever. A clown jumping on one end provides the force to push the other clown up into the air.

△ A wheelbarrow is a simple machine that uses a lever and a wheel to move things. Have you ever used a wheelbarrow to make moving things easier?

Light and colour

Sunlight is a kind of energy which comes from the Sun. It travels through Space as light waves. Sunlight seems to be colourless or white. But really it is made up of several colours mixed together.

▽ You can see the colours of sunlight in a rainbow. Light passing through raindrops is split up into red, orange, yellow, green, blue, indigo and violet.

▽ Things are different colours. This is because they soak up some of the colours from light and let the others bounce off them.

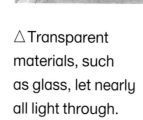

△ Transparent materials, such as glass, let nearly all light through.

△ Translucent materials, such as plastic, let some light through.

△ Opaque materials, such as wrapping paper, do not let any light through.

◁ A tomato soaks up all colours except red, which bounces back off it, into our eyes. So we see a red tomato.

Make a rainbow

You can split up light into different colours. On a sunny day, fill a tub with water and put it by a window. Rest a flat mirror against one side of the tub. Angle the mirror to catch the sunlight until a rainbow appears on the ceiling. You could use plasticine to hold the mirror in place once you have made the rainbow.

△ Sunlight travels through Space very quickly. Nothing travels faster than light.

△ At night there is only starlight and moonlight. Long ago, people used fire for light.

△ Later, people used wax candles and oil lamps. Now we mainly use electricity.

Rain's son, the Rainbow
(An Australian folk tale)

Rainbow was Rain's son. He only came out to stop his father from falling from the sky. People had to chase Rainbow away to allow Rain to fall, otherwise there would be a drought.

Word box
Transparent materials let most light pass through.
Translucent materials only let some light through.
Opaque materials do not let any light through.

429

Shadows

Light waves travel in straight lines. They cannot bend around things. If something gets in the way of a light wave, it blocks the light and casts a shadow. The Earth spins as it goes around the Sun. This makes outdoor shadows point in different directions and change length at different times of the day.

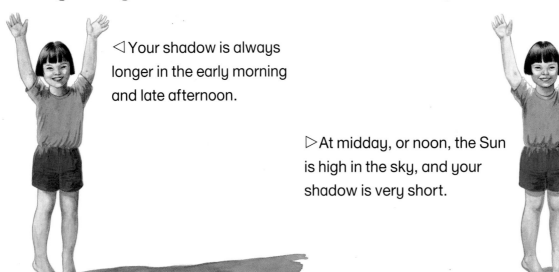

Find the answers

When is your shadow longest?

When is the Sun high in the sky?

◁ Your shadow is always longer in the early morning and late afternoon.

▷ At midday, or noon, the Sun is high in the sky, and your shadow is very short.

dog   rabbit

giraffe   bird

Make shadow shapes
In a darkened room, ask a friend to shine a torch onto a wall beside you. Make sure your hands are in between the light rays and the wall. By holding your hands as shown here, you can cast different animal-shaped shadows.

430

Reflections

When light hits any smooth, shiny surface, it bounces back making a reflection. When you look into a mirror, light bounces off your body, then off the mirror back at you, so you can see your reflection.

The light from the Sun bounces off the Moon, giving us moonlight.

▷ Lots of shiny surfaces reflect light. This boy can see his reflection in an empty saucepan. Can you see yourself in any objects at home?

△ Mirrors are made of a sheet of glass in front of a thin piece of shiny metal.

△ Moonlight is light reflected from the Sun. It is sometimes reflected again in the shiny surface of water.

The Rain Puddle
(A story by Adelaide Holl)

The farmyard animals see their own reflections in a rain puddle and think there are other animals drowning in it. When the sun comes out and dries up the puddle, they foolishly think the reflected animals have been saved.

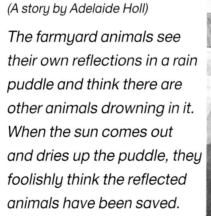

Refraction and lenses

If you put a straw in a glass of water, it seems to bend. This is called refraction. Refraction is caused by light travelling at different speeds. Light moves faster through air than it does through water. When it changes speed it can change direction too.

Lenses use refraction. They are specially shaped to bend light and make things seem smaller and further away, or bigger and closer.

△ Refraction can make things look bigger. A goldfish in a round, glass bowl seems to grow as it swims towards you.

▽ The lens in a telescope can help you to see distant stars.

zoom lens

△ You can photograph things that are far away and make them look nearer with the zoom lens of a camera.

△ The lenses in a pair of binoculars help you to see things that are far away.

△ If you put a straw in a glass, it seems to change shape and size because of refraction.

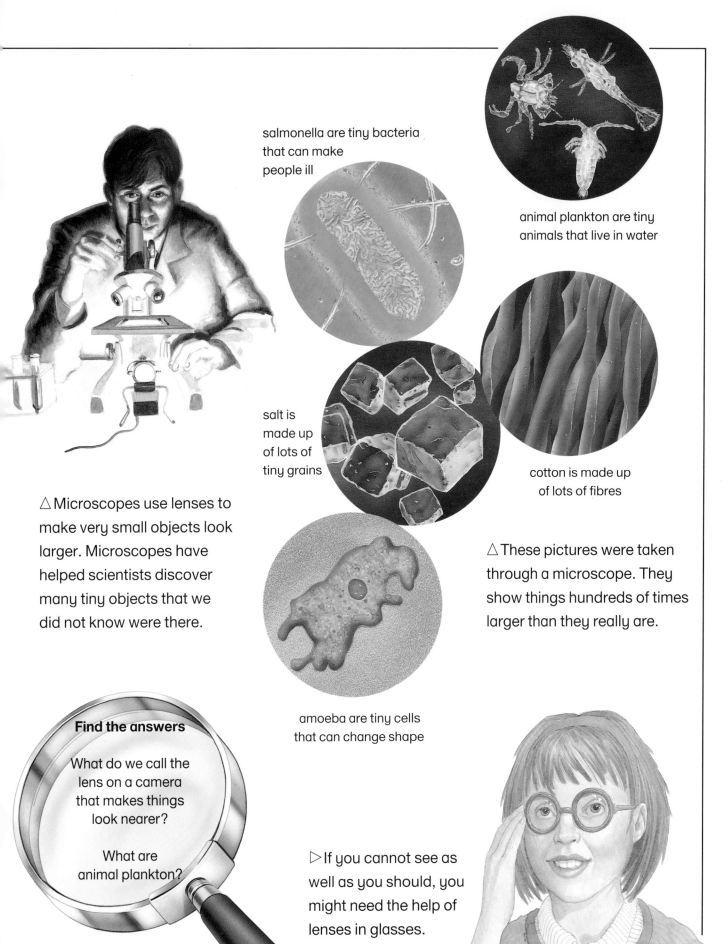

salmonella are tiny bacteria that can make people ill

animal plankton are tiny animals that live in water

salt is made up of lots of tiny grains

cotton is made up of lots of fibres

△ Microscopes use lenses to make very small objects look larger. Microscopes have helped scientists discover many tiny objects that we did not know were there.

△ These pictures were taken through a microscope. They show things hundreds of times larger than they really are.

amoeba are tiny cells that can change shape

Find the answers

What do we call the lens on a camera that makes things look nearer?

What are animal plankton?

▷ If you cannot see as well as you should, you might need the help of lenses in glasses.

Sound

Every noise you hear is made by something vibrating, or moving backwards and forwards very quickly.

Sound travels in waves. Sound waves need to have something to move through. They can travel through solids, liquids or gases.

△ Sound travels through the air at about 1,224 kilometres an hour. Concorde is supersonic, it can travel faster than sound.

▽ When someone speaks to you, vibrations pass through their mouth into the air, making the air vibrate. The vibrations travel to your ear in sound waves and you hear them as sound.

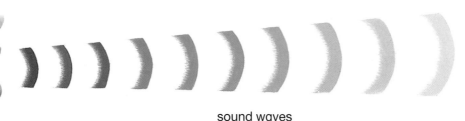

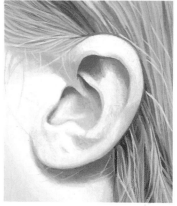

sound waves

Seeing sounds

You cannot see sound waves, but you can see their effects. Make a drum by stretching foil tightly over a bowl. Attach with a rubber band. Put some grains of uncooked rice on the drum. Then bang on the lid of a tin. The sound waves will make the rice bounce.

▽ Lightning and thunder happen at the same time, but we see lightning before we hear thunder. This is because sound travels more slowly than light.

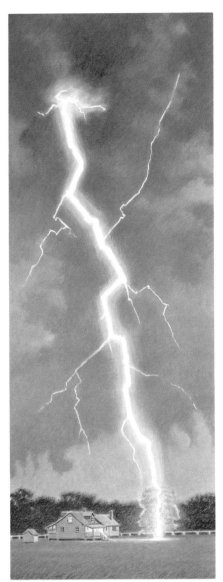

△ Sound travels faster and further through water than air. Whales sing to each other. They can hear each other's songs from up to 100 kilometres away.

△ You can hear sound that has travelled through a solid by putting your ear to a table, and asking a friend to bang a saucepan at the other end.

Word box
Vibrations are fast, regular backwards and forwards movements in solids, liquids and gases.
Sound waves are produced by vibrations. They carry sounds at different speeds through solids, liquids and gases.

High and low

Some sounds are higher than others. The more vibrations there are in a second, the higher the sound. So there are fewer vibrations in low sounds than high sounds.

Humans hear sounds between 20 and 20,000 vibrations a second, but some animals can hear higher sounds.

△ This man is playing a double bass, which makes a low sound. The boy is making a high sound with his tin whistle.

▽ The numbers below tell you how many vibrations each of these animals can hear in a second.

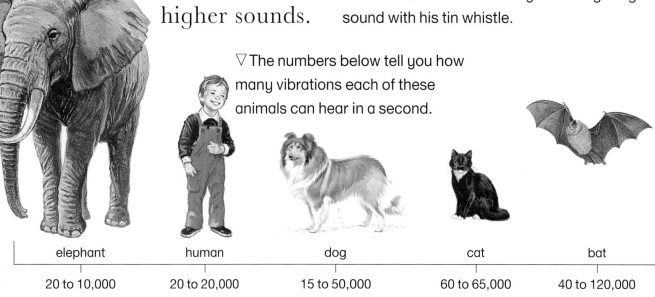

elephant	human	dog	cat	bat
20 to 10,000	20 to 20,000	15 to 50,000	60 to 65,000	40 to 120,000

▷ Female opera singers usually have higher voices than male opera singers. The higher the voice, the higher the number of vibrations in a second.

436

How loud?

The loudness of a sound depends on the size of the sound waves. Big sound waves are louder than smaller ones.

Loudness is measured in decibels. A sound that can only just be heard measures one decibel. We whisper at about 20 decibels. Blue whales can sing at 188 decibels, which is louder than any other animal.

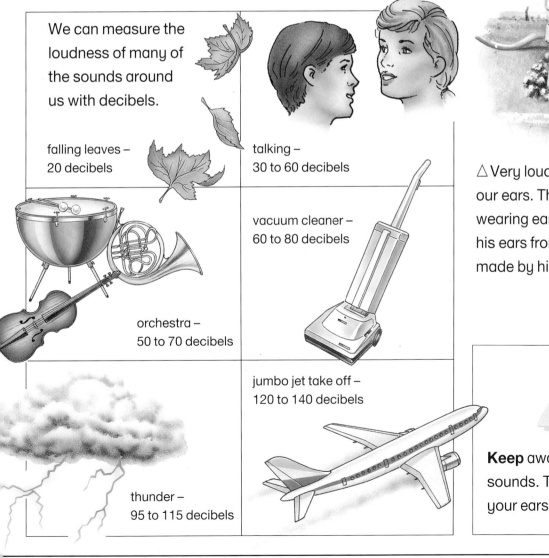

We can measure the loudness of many of the sounds around us with decibels.

falling leaves – 20 decibels

talking – 30 to 60 decibels

vacuum cleaner – 60 to 80 decibels

orchestra – 50 to 70 decibels

jumbo jet take off – 120 to 140 decibels

thunder – 95 to 115 decibels

△ Very loud noises can harm our ears. This workman is wearing ear muffs to protect his ears from the loud sound made by his pneumatic drill.

Keep away from very loud sounds. They can damage your ears.

Echoes

An echo is the sound you hear when sound waves reflect back from a wall or another hard object.

It takes the sound waves a certain amount of time to hit the walls and bounce back again. By measuring this time, we can find out how far away something is. This is how submarines find things on the seafloor.

sound waves

△ The sound waves made by this girl's voice have bounced off the mountain wall, so she can hear her echo.

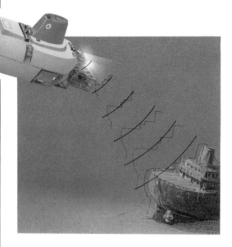

△ This mini-sub sends out sound waves, measures the echoes' time and records where the shipwreck is below.

Echo's fate
(A Roman myth)

Echo was one of the great goddess Juno's maids. She got into trouble for talking too much and almost lost her voice. Later, she fell in love with Narcissus but he did not return her love. Broken hearted, she changed into a stone and was only able to repeat words that others said first, just like an echo.

◁ If you shout into an empty bucket, your voice bounces off the sides, loudly.

▷ Swiflets call out and use echoes to find their way in dark caves.

Making music

One of the most wonderful things about sound is music. Different people think of different things as music. Some people hear music in a babbling brook or the wind rustling through leaves. Others prefer music made by musical instruments. It is easy to make simple instruments and form a band.

△ This boy has made a shaker by putting dried peas into two plastic pots. It rattles when he shakes it up and down.

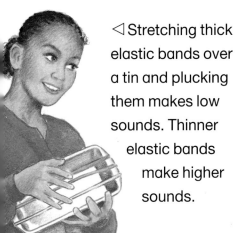

◁ Stretching thick elastic bands over a tin and plucking them makes low sounds. Thinner elastic bands make higher sounds.

▽ Blowing down different lengths of drinking straws, stuck onto card, makes the sound of Pan pipes.

△ A scraper can easily be made from an empty, ridged plastic bottle and a pencil.

▽ A piece of thin paper wrapped around a comb sounds like a harmonica when it is blown hard.

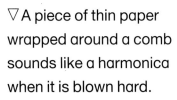

▷ These children are playing a tune using their home-made musical instruments.

Everyday science

Your bike is full of science! It uses many of the scientific ideas already explained. Look at the bike below and the science that each different part uses.

△ The frame is made of strong metal. Its shape is made of triangles, which make the structure strong.

▷The cyclist uses her energy to push the pedals, which move the bike forward.

the helmet is streamlined so air does not hold the cyclist back

the bell rings to make a warning sound

◁ The bicycle lamp is powered by a battery.

▷Air is pumped into the tyres to keep up the pressure.

the lamp helps the cyclist to see and be seen in the dark

▽ Oil is used to reduce friction, so the bike's parts run smoothly.

tyre

brake pad

△ The brakes use friction to slow down the wheels.

People and Places

Where do people live?

The world we live in is made up of many different environments, or surroundings. These include deserts, grasslands, woodlands, rainforests and mountains. Some of these areas are shown on the map. People can live in almost every area.

Since early times, people have built homes with natural materials that grew or were found close by. Today, many homes are built with materials made in factories.

▽ Inuit people in North America used igloos as homes. Igloos were built of blocks of snow.

Key to map

hot desert		evergreen forest	
grassland		deciduous wood	
cold desert		rainforest	
		mountains	

△ People live in reed houses on Lake Titicaca in South America. They are built on a floor of flattened reeds.

Word box
Environments are our surroundings. They affect the way we live.
Manufactured materials are made in a factory.

442

▽ About 300 years ago, many European homes had thatched roofs made of straw. Thatching is still done today.

Factory materials
Materials such as glass, concrete, bricks, steel and strong plastics are used to build homes all over the world. These materials are manufactured, which means they are made in a factory.

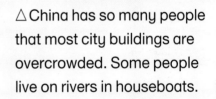

△ China has so many people that most city buildings are overcrowded. Some people live on rivers in houseboats.

△ In many parts of Africa, mud and straw are easy to come by. So mud houses with thatched roofs are popular.

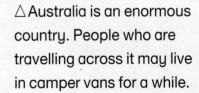

△ Australia is an enormous country. People who are travelling across it may live in camper vans for a while.

Languages

Language is made up of spoken and written words. Without words it would be difficult for us to tell others what we mean. We would have to act out what we were trying to say, which would take a long time. It is hard to understand people from other countries, because they use different words to say the same thing.

Whispering game

One player whispers to a neighbour. They repeat what was said to the person next to them, and so on. The last person says it out loud. Usually, the words have changed.

▷Throughout the world, hands are used in different ways as a greeting, and as a sign of welcome and respect.

▽The children below are all saying good morning. The different languages are written above them. How many do you know?

你好嗎

সুপ্রভাত

günaydın

안녕

Buenos días

おはよう

你好嗎

שָׁלוֹם, בֹּקֶר טוֹב

здрáвствуи

jamm nga fënaan

नमस्कार

GOOD MORNING

صَباح الخَير ~ أهلاً

καλημέρα

မင်္ဂလာပါ၊ ဆရာ။

BONJOUR!

Religious beliefs

Many things have happened in the world that we do not understand. Religious beliefs are one way of helping to explain them. Most religions have a god or gods and laws to tell people how to behave. Some people's special religious buildings are shown here.

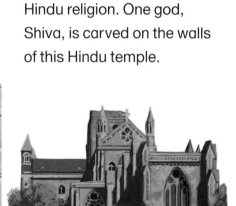

△ There are many gods in the Hindu religion. One god, Shiva, is carved on the walls of this Hindu temple.

△ Buddhists follow the sayings of the Buddha. They worship in a temple.

△ In Jerusalem, The Western Wall is visited by Jews, who believe in one god only.

△ Christians worship one god and Jesus Christ in chapels, churches and cathedrals.

△ Shinto symbols are important to Japanese people who worship gods of nature.

◁ All Muslims try to visit this holy city of Mecca. The Muslim name for god is Allah.

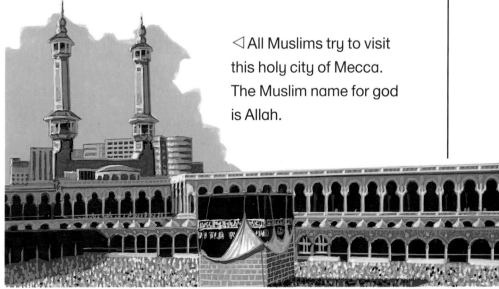

Food from far and wide

All kinds of delicious foods are grown throughout the world. Different types of weather, called climate, help to decide how people live and what sort of food they grow.

Once, certain foods were only eaten by the people who grew them. Today, food can be transported to markets all over the world for us to buy. How many of the foods below do you know?

Make a fruit salad
Buy some brightly coloured fruits and wash them. Ask an adult to cut them into cubes and slices. Place in a bowl and mix together. Add a little fresh fruit juice.

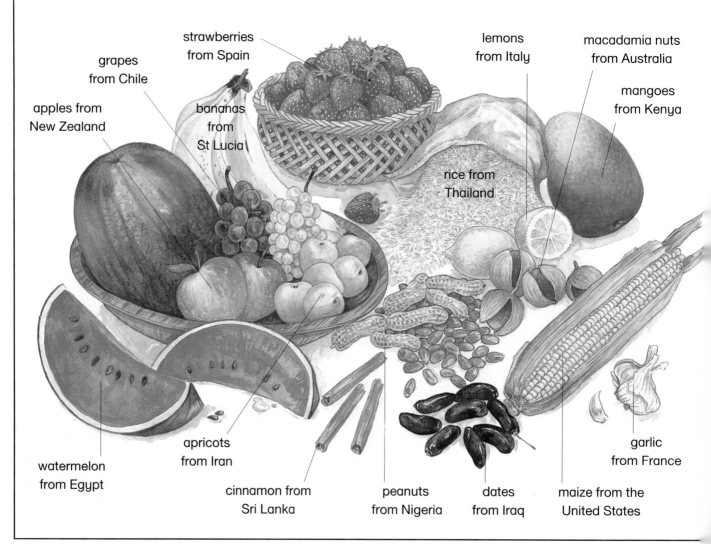

strawberries from Spain

grapes from Chile

apples from New Zealand

bananas from St Lucia

lemons from Italy

macadamia nuts from Australia

mangoes from Kenya

rice from Thailand

watermelon from Egypt

apricots from Iran

cinnamon from Sri Lanka

peanuts from Nigeria

dates from Iraq

maize from the United States

garlic from France

Sports and games

People all over the world play sports and games all through the year. Some are played alone, while others are played with a partner or in teams. Football and hockey are games that are played against people in many countries, to decide which country's team is the winner. Which sports and games do you enjoy playing?

△ Ice hockey is a fast and tough game.

△ Volleyball is played on beaches worldwide.

▽ Every four years, sports men and women from different countries meet to play against each other at the Olympic games. The winners are given medals.

△ In Katanga, Zaire, children play a game of marbles using fruits.

▷ Children and adults all over the world enjoy kicking a ball and playing football.

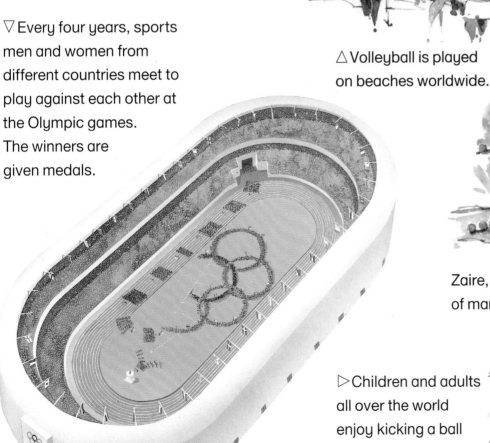

Traditions

A tradition is something that is done in the same way, year after year. It may be a celebration, a storytelling or a way of making something. Different places and groups of people have their own traditional festivals, stories and crafts.

In the following pages, we will be looking at five large areas of the world: the Americas, Europe, Africa, Asia and Australasia and the Pacific Islands. Each is made up of many countries that all have their own traditions.

△ For thousands of years, African people have made models out of clay, wood and gold. This head is made of red clay. It was made in west Africa about 800 years ago.

◁ Every year, people in Belgium, Europe, dress up as giants for a parade around the town streets. Each costume has a peephole, so the person inside can see where they are going. Can you see the people's faces in this picture?

Snowmaiden
(A Russian folk tale)

Once upon a time, a couple who longed to have a child carved a young girl out of snow. When she magically came alive they were delighted and called her Snowmaiden.

▷These traditional rod puppets are from Java, in Asia. They are made of wood and used to tell stories. A puppeteer works them by moving the long sticks attached to their bodies.

△ The Aborigine people in Australia tell their children wonderful stories as they paint Dreamtime pictures. The children learn to paint the pictures and remember the stories so they can tell them to their own children one day. This way, the stories will never be forgotten.

▷For hundreds of years, people have ridden horses to round up their cattle in America. Today, cowgirls and cowboys show off their horse-riding skills to crowds of people at shows called rodeos. They are popular in the United States and Canada.

449

The Americas

For hundreds of years, the Americas have drawn people from all over the world. Amazing landscapes and different climates still attract millions of visitors each year. Some decide to stay after their holiday. All of these peoples add to the richness and colourful style of American life.

△ The area called the Americas is shown in red.

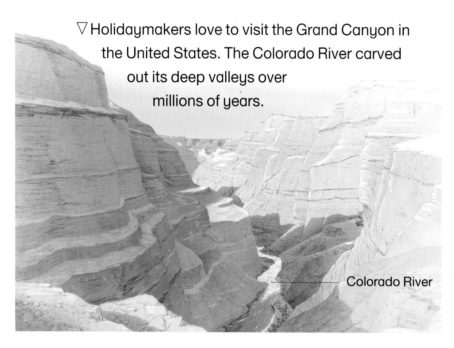

▽ Holidaymakers love to visit the Grand Canyon in the United States. The Colorado River carved out its deep valleys over millions of years.

Colorado River

△ Many people go to see the famous Statue of Liberty, in New York City.

▷ Fruit and vegetables are sold in this busy market, high in the Andes mountains.

△ The Horseshoe Falls in Canada are part of the group of waterfalls called Niagara Falls. Some of the falls are in Canada, the rest are in the United States.

▽ Sugar Loaf mountain rises above the bay in Rio de Janeiro, Brazil. The city is a lively place to live, surrounded by magnificent views.

△ Alaska is the northernmost state of the United States. Much of the land is frozen with massive rivers of ice, called glaciers.

Word box
Glaciers are huge rivers of ice that move very slowly down valleys. They follow the easiest way to the sea.
Canyons are deep, steep-sided valleys. They are usually in dry areas where the sides do not get worn away by the beating rain.

451

The frozen north

The Inuit people came from Asia to Canada thousands of years ago. The early Inuits used dog sleds for transport and made homes from snow or animal skins. There was no soil for growing food, so they hunted caribou and seals for food and clothing. Today, some Inuits hunt, but most work in offices and factories.

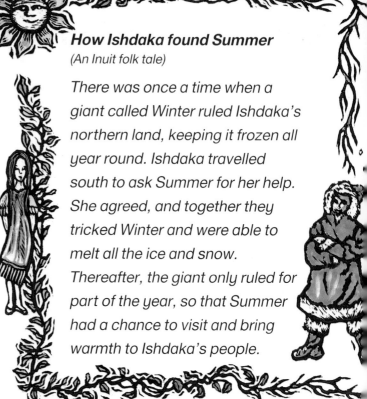

How Ishdaka found Summer
(An Inuit folk tale)

There was once a time when a giant called Winter ruled Ishdaka's northern land, keeping it frozen all year round. Ishdaka travelled south to ask Summer for her help. She agreed, and together they tricked Winter and were able to melt all the ice and snow. Thereafter, the giant only ruled for part of the year, so that Summer had a chance to visit and bring warmth to Ishdaka's people.

△ Rubbing noses is an Inuit sign of affection, like a kiss.

◁ Inuits catch fish to eat. This man is spearing fish through an ice hole.

▷ Today, most Inuits live in wooden houses and drive snow mobiles and cars. Planes bring supplies and medicines.

snow mobile

Native Americans

Native Americans were the first people to live in North America. They spoke many languages and hunted, fished and farmed. When Europeans arrived, Native Americans were forced to live in areas known as reservations.

△ The Pueblo people are Native Americans. They dance and sing at the maize festival to make the rains come and bring them a good harvest.

▷ The medicine man uses magic to help heal sick people. He draws magic signs in the sand and chants.

▽ White settlers from Europe first arrived over 350 years ago. At first, they were friends with the Native Americans, but later fought many wars against them.

Find the answers

Who were the first people to live in North America?

What does the medicine man use to help heal people?

△ Trees are cut down by forest workers called lumberjacks. They use power saws.

Forestry

British Columbia in Canada is one of the world's largest timber producers. Timber is wood from trees. It is needed to make building materials, furniture and paper.

The Columbian forests are looked after carefully, so that new tree seedlings are always growing to replace the trees that are cut down.

△ Huge trucks take the trees away to sawmills. Then the bark is removed from the trees and they are sawn into planks.

◁ Trunks of maple trees are drilled to collect a watery sap. When this is boiled it turns into the sweet, sticky liquid known as maple syrup.

Find the answers

What is made from timber?

Where is British Columbia?

▷ Maple syrup is delicious on waffles and pancakes.

Cattle ranches

North American farmers keep cattle on big farms called ranches. Cattle over nine months old are kept in fenced off areas and fed on special food to make them grow bigger. Lassos are used to round up the cattle.

◁ The South American cowboy is called a gaucho. He wears a broad hat, baggy trousers, a decorated belt and spurs on his boots.

spurs

Make a gaucho hat
Cut a circle of card with a hole the size of your head. Cut a strip of card 4 cm wide, to make a headband. Cut edges of band, as shown. Tape ends to fit your head. Fold bottom edges and glue over hole. Cut a circle the size of your headband and glue on top.

▽ Cattle in North America have been rounded up on horseback since the early days of the Wild West.

lasso

◁ On some large ranches, trucks and helicopters are used to find lost cattle.

West Indies

The West Indies is made up of thousands of islands in the Caribbean Sea. Cuba is the largest of these islands.

Bananas, coconuts, coffee, cotton, tobacco and sugar cane grow well in the warm weather on these islands.

It is sunny all year round, so people can work and relax outside.

▽ Puerto Rico is an island in the West Indies. Puerto Rican fishermen go out to sea in small boats. They often have to mend nets that have ripped on rocks below the sea.

Make Caribbean bananas

Peel some bananas. Ask an adult to cut them into two. For each, mix two tablespoons of orange juice with a teaspoon of lemon juice and two teaspoons of brown sugar. Pour on top. Sprinkle a tablespoon of coconut over each. Ask an adult to grill them for five minutes.

Find the answers

Which is the largest island in the West Indies?

What grows well in the West Indies?

Amazon Indians

Amazon Indians live in the South American rainforests. They look after the forest because it gives them all the food, medicine and building materials they need.

Other people are not looking after the land. They are cutting down many of the trees to sell as timber or to make space for new farms.

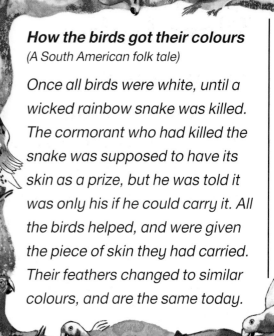

How the birds got their colours
(A South American folk tale)

Once all birds were white, until a wicked rainbow snake was killed. The cormorant who had killed the snake was supposed to have its skin as a prize, but he was told it was only his if he could carry it. All the birds helped, and were given the piece of skin they had carried. Their feathers changed to similar colours, and are the same today.

▽ Many Amazon Indians sleep in hammocks and cook food outside.

△ These men are fishing with a bow and arrow. They must have sharp eyes and move quickly to catch fish this way.

◁ The forest people live in clearings. They get all their food from the forest and rivers. Hunters often go away for many days at a time.

457

Mexico

More people live in Mexico City, Mexico's busy capital, than in any other city in the world. Other Mexican towns are quieter, especially during the hottest part of the day, when most people rest.

Many visitors travel to Mexico to see the amazing temples that were built by the Aztecs.

△ The Aztecs lived in Mexico hundreds of years ago. Their capital, Tenochtitlán, probably looked like this. The ruins of these temples are visited by people today.

▽ It is noon, the hottest part of the day, in this small Mexican town. Many people have gone inside to rest, away from the sun. Others take a break from their work and sit in the shade under the cool arches in the town square.

Find the answers

What is Mexico's capital city?

Why do most people rest at noon?

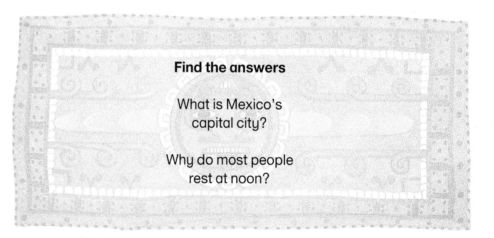

Traditions

Carnival, Thanksgiving and the Canadian Winter Festival are just a few of the many traditions that take place in the Americas today. They are happy times, when people celebrate with their friends, family and neighbours.

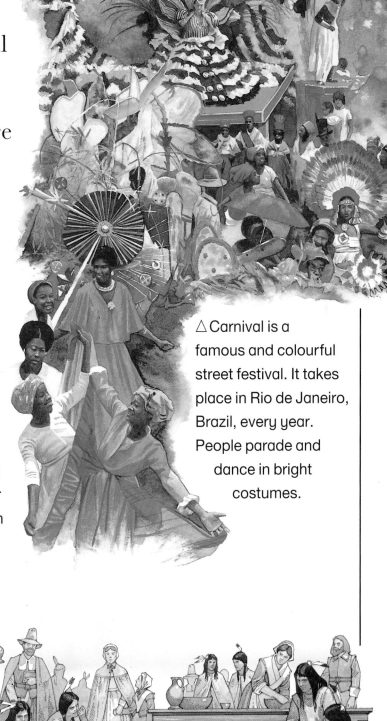

△ Each year, a giant ice palace is built for the Winter Festival in Quebec, Canada.

△ Carnival is a famous and colourful street festival. It takes place in Rio de Janeiro, Brazil, every year. People parade and dance in bright costumes.

▷ Thanksgiving is the United State's favourite tradition. The first Thanksgiving was a huge party thrown by settlers, to thank the Native Americans for showing them how to farm their new land.

Europe

Europe is made up of many countries. The northernmost areas in the Arctic are cold and snowy all year round. In the south, by the Mediterranean Sea, it can be very hot and dry.

People from northern Europe, such as Scandinavia, are often fair skinned with light hair. People from southern Europe, such as Italy, are usually darker.

△ Europe's many countries make up the red shape shown on this map.

◁ People from all over the world visit the Mediterranean countries to lie in the sun on sandy beaches and swim in the warm, blue sea.

▽ Iceland has many geysers. They blast hot water into the air, every now and then.

△ Some Sami, or Lapp people, keep reindeer. They take them further south in the spring. On the way, they live in tents called lavos.

▷St Basil's church in Moscow, Russia, is famous for its many brightly coloured, onion-shaped domes. Russia is such a large country, that it stretches across both Europe and Asia. Moscow is in Europe.

▽ Prague, the capital of the Czech Republic, is full of many old and beautiful buildings. It is called the city of 100 spires because it has so many churches.

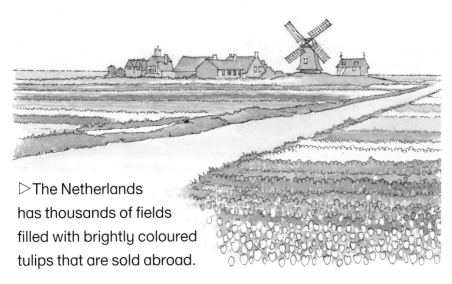

▷The Netherlands has thousands of fields filled with brightly coloured tulips that are sold abroad.

△ Edinburgh Castle in Scotland stands high above the city on a volcanic rock.

Word box
Geysers are hot springs that throw up jets of hot water. In volcanic areas, hot water underground turns to steam and pushes out into the air. **Mediterranean** areas include all the lands surrounding the Mediterranean Sea.

461

Farming

Some European farmers keep animals, others grow crops, many do both.

Machines can be used to plant and harvest crops on flatter land. Farming hilly ground is more difficult. These areas are often used to graze sheep and goats.

Make a sheep picture
Draw a sheep using this shape as a guide. Colour in its face and legs. Glue cotton wool onto its back. Glue used match sticks to make a sheep pen, as shown.

▽A lot of wheat is grown in Europe. Tractors and combine harvesters gather in the crop towards the end of summer.

△ On a small farm, everyone helps to look after the animals. The chickens are given grain to eat and their eggs are collected each day.

△ Many farms in Spain grow grapes. The grapes are cut in September, and are mostly made into wine.

Fishing

The fishing industry in Europe is huge. Thousands of tons of fish are sent to the fish markets every day.

Shellfish, such as lobsters and crabs, are trapped in baskets. Other fish are caught by floating nets.

Find the answers

What are large fishing boats called?

How are shellfish caught?

▽ Fishing is often a family business. These two Greek brothers fish every day. Sometimes they hire out their boat to holidaymakers.

△ These fishermen are from Brittany, in France. They go out to sea for several days in large boats. They sell the fish they catch in a fish market in their home port.

▷ Large fishing boats are called trawlers. The fishermen on this Russian trawler will freeze the fish on board to keep it fresh until they return.

Mountains

Europe has many beautiful mountains. In Norway, inlets of sea, called fjords, cut into mountainous coastlines. The world-famous Alps stretch through many countries. Hundreds of people climb and ski on them every year.

Dogs to the rescue!
The St Bernard dog is named after the St Bernard monastery in the Swiss Alps. Many years ago, the monks in this monastery reared and trained these dogs to rescue people trapped on the mountains in snow blizzards.

▷The countries of Scandinavia have warm summers. People on holiday sometimes bathe in low mountain lakes. They also take special baths, called saunas, inside wooden cabins.

◁These people have come to a ski resort for their holiday. Those who are used to skiing will climb the mountain in a chair lift and ski down. Beginners will ski on gentle slopes, or practise on flatter areas in the resort's village. Others prefer to sled or toboggan.

Traditions

As Europe is made up of so many countries, there are hundreds of different festivals and celebrations.

Certain festivals, such as New Year, are celebrated by groups of people everywhere. Some traditions belong to one area or country only.

△ In Switzerland, there is an opening parade every autumn for the onion festival.

△ Russian dancing is famous throughout the world. The dancers have to be very fit and strong. They kick their legs out while squatting, leap high in the air and touch their toes.

△ In Italy, over 300 years ago, a puppet called Pulcinella became so well loved, the show spread to France. From there it went to England, where Pulcinella became Mr Punch.

465

Africa

Africa is an area of many landscapes and climates. It includes tropical rainforests and the world's largest and hottest desert, the Sahara.

Three-quarters of Africans live in the countryside, earning their living by farming. More and more people are moving to the cities to work in shops, offices and factories.

△ Africa is shown in red. It is made up of many countries.

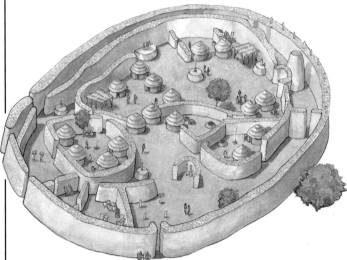

◁ About 900 years ago, the Shona people built the city of Great Zimbabwe in southern Africa. Its ruins are still there today.

Word box
Safaris are journeys into the wild to see and photograph wild animals in their natural surroundings.
Pyramids were built in Egypt thousands of years ago as places to bury important people when they died.

▷ In Morocco, north Africa, the old part of some towns have walls around them. Souks, or town markets, are within these walls.

◁ In ancient Egypt, Pharaohs, or kings, were buried in pyramid tombs with their treasure.

▽ There are many open markets in west Africa. These women are carrying the shopping home on their heads.

△ Some African towns are on rivers, so boats can be used to carry people and goods.

△ Once people on safari shot large African animals. Nowadays, they take photographs instead.

Village and nomadic life

In the towns, many people live in modern houses built from manufactured materials. In the villages, houses are often made of sun-dried mud with roofs of straw or leaves.

Tuareg and Masai people do not live in towns or villages. They live a nomadic life, which means they travel from place to place.

△ This Tuareg man is lowering a bucket on a rope to scoop water from a well below the desert sand.

▽ The Tuareg people wander the Sahara Desert with their camels and goats. Their homes are tents carried on the camels' backs.

△ Camels are used to carry goods across the desert. They can travel for days without a drink.

Snake magic
(A folk tale from east Africa)

A poor, hungry woman and her son helped a snake. They were rewarded with a magic ring and a casket that always gave them a home, riches and delicious food.

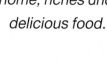

△ In many African villages, women prepare meals together outside their homes. They pound millet or cassava into flour.

▷ The greatest day in a young Masai warrior's life is when he becomes a junior elder. Young women dress up in colourful beaded collars for the warrior's procession.

△ Bridges made from branches and vines cross some rivers. They look wobbly, but local people use them easily.

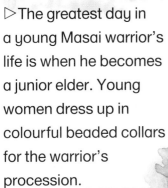

◁ Masai women build a holy house, called an osinkira, for the young warrior's ceremony. An altar inside it is made from three wooden stakes cut from sacred trees. The house is always burned afterwards.

Farming

In some parts of Africa modern machinery is used to farm the land, but most farmers use simple tools. In eastern and southern grassland areas, peanuts, maize and millet are grown. In warm, wet areas, bananas, rice and yams grow well. Coffee, cocoa beans, coconuts and cotton are grown mainly to sell abroad.

△ Ostriches are very strong and can be ridden like horses. They can give a nasty kick if they are in a bad mood!

△ Ostriches are kept in South Africa for their eggs, feathers and meat. The females have special shelters where they lay their eggs.

▽ In Zaire, central Africa, the farmers grow tea bushes on hillsides. The leaves are picked by hand. They are dried before being packed.

▽ Coffee plants produce fruits called berries. Each berry has two beans. Some of these are roasted and ground to make coffee powder.

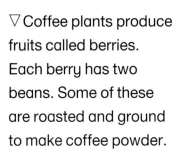

Find the answers

Why are ostriches kept in South Africa?

In which part of Africa are peanuts grown?

▽ Some farmers are lucky enough to have land near Africa's longest river, the river Nile. Waterwheel pumps, worked by animals, keep the Nile's water flowing along ditches to water crops.

Make an ostrich
Draw an ostrich onto card, using this shape as a guide. Colour it in. Glue on a bead for its eye.

Cut out feather shapes from black and white paper. Cut edges, as shown. Glue the feathers onto your ostrich's body.

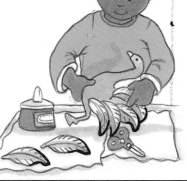

471

Life on the water

Some people in Africa live in villages by the sea and rivers. There are few streets, but people move about easily in small boats.

The houses are built on high stilts, so that when the river rises during the rainy season, the houses are kept dry. Children here are more used to water than dry land!

Make a stilt house
Cut and fold the ends of four tubes, as shown. Tape to the bottom of a cardboard box. Fold a piece of card in half. Tape over box to make roof. Paint doors and windows. Glue straws onto the roof.

▷ This is a fishing village in Benin, west Africa. Local people can buy vegetables and fruit from boats that visit their homes.

The pumpkin boat
(A folk tale from Madagascar)

One day a pumpkin fell into the river. A group of small animals thought it would make a wonderful boat to sail down river. But Rat became hungry and secretly began to nibble the bottom. When water flooded in, the boat tipped over and all the animals had to swim for the shore. They were all very angry with Rat!

Traditions

Many of the African countries are famous for their traditional crafts. Beautiful masks and colourful materials have been made in the same way for thousands of years.

There are also exciting festivals and celebrations all over Africa.

△ This colourful cloth is from Ghana in west Africa. It is woven from dyed cotton. Traditional clothes in Africa often have bright colours and bold patterns.

◁ African people have made masks out of materials such as clay, wood, bronze and gold for thousands of years. This mask was made in central Africa. It was used for special ceremonies.

◁ Every year, men from Argungu in Nigeria hold a fishing festival. They fish for giant perches, using dried gourds, or calabashes, as floats.

473

Asia

Asia covers a vast area. Its lands vary from freezing Siberia in the north to warm, tropical India and Thailand in the southeast.

Over half of the people in the world live in Asia. Many of them live in busy cities. Very few people live in the dry desert and rocky mountain areas.

△ Asia's enormous land area is shown in red.

▷ Many people living in the Middle East are Muslim. They worship in a mosque, like this one in Dubai. It looks spectacular when it is lit up at night.

▽ These Hindus are bathing in the holy waters of the river Ganges in Varanasi, northern India.

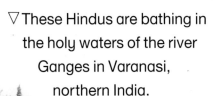

△ Over half of Thailand is covered in teak forest. Teak is a very important timber tree. Elephants move the teak logs to the river, where they are floated down to the sawmills in the capital city, Bangkok.

◁ There are many bazaars, or markets, in Afghanistan. People from the hills and mountains come to sell their goods.

△ China's city streets are busy. Bicycles are often the quickest way to travel around.

△ The Himalayas are the highest mountain range in the world. Many people try to climb them every year.

◁ The Great Wall of China was built over 1,000 years ago to protect China. It is the longest wall in the world.

Word box
Teak timber comes from forests in Southeast Asia. It polishes well, so is used to make furniture.
Bazaars are eastern markets where goods are sold or swapped.

Different ways of life

Most Asian people live and work in villages, towns or cities, but some people choose to lead a different way of life. This may be because they have special beliefs, such as the Buddhist monks. Other people, such as some Mongolian and Tibetan families travel around to work. A few of the unusual ways of life in Asia are shown on this page.

△ These people are from Mongolia. They wander the grassy plains with their animals. Their homes are felt tents, called yurts.

◁ On the slopes of the Himalayan mountains, Buddhist monks live in monasteries. They have chosen to live apart from other people, so they can pray and study in peace.

▷In Israel there are farms called kibbutzim. Everyone works together to grow food for the people of the kibbutz and to sell at markets. Here, workers are picking oranges.

◁This is a whole village under one roof. The Iban people of Sarawak, Malaysia, often live in a longhouse like this. Inside, as many as 70 families have separate rooms, off a long corridor.

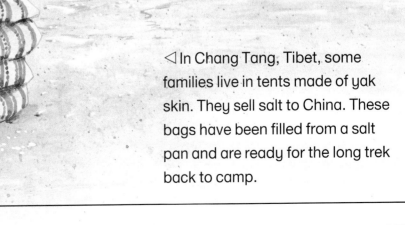

◁In Chang Tang, Tibet, some families live in tents made of yak skin. They sell salt to China. These bags have been filled from a salt pan and are ready for the long trek back to camp.

Industry

People who manufacture, or make, similar products are said to work in the same industry. There are a huge number of industries in Asia. Some Asian industries make very complicated electrical goods. Others are simple industries, such as farming rice, cotton and tea.

△ Rice grows best in flooded fields, so all of the work has to be done by hand or with the help of animals.

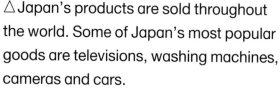

△ Japan's products are sold throughout the world. Some of Japan's most popular goods are televisions, washing machines, cameras and cars.

crystallized ginger

▽ Spices help to make food taste and smell good. Many spices are grown and used in Asia.

ginger root

coriander

coriander leaves

slice of ginger root

ground black pepper

whole black peppercorns

△ Oil is one of Asia's biggest industries.
Over half the world's oil is found in Asia, with
a quarter of it mined in Saudi Arabia alone.

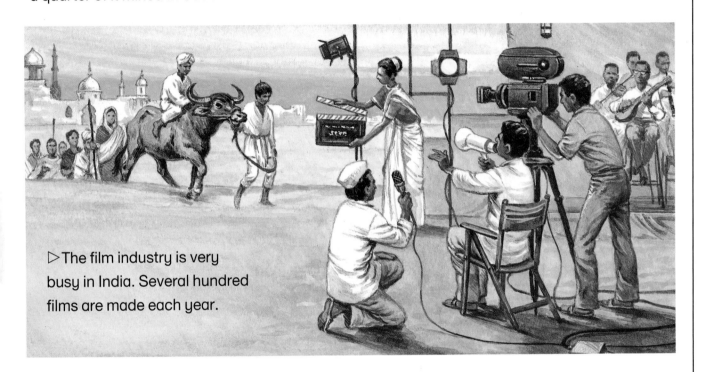

▷ The film industry is very
busy in India. Several hundred
films are made each year.

Weave a rug

Fold a piece of thin card
in half. Cut slits, as
shown. Open out. Tape
strips of coloured paper
to one edge. Weave strips
in and out until you reach the
end. Tape in place. Weave strips
until you have a colourful rug.

▽ Woven Persian rugs
are famous around
the world.

Traditions

There are many celebrations and traditions to be found throughout the different countries in Asia. All are fun to watch or take part in. You can see people dressing up in costumes, an exciting fireworks display and a colourful painting on these pages. Perhaps you have been lucky enough to see some of them before.

△ Islamic art is based on the Muslim religion. Many beautiful patterns and designs are created.

▽ During the Chinese New Year, some adults dress in a dragon costume and dance through the streets collecting gifts for those in need.

▽ On the island of Bali, in Indonesia, the women and children offer gifts of flowers and fruit to the gods, to help protect their villages.

Make a Bun Bang Fai picture
Draw a firework picture with wax crayons. Use your brightest colours and draw plenty of rockets. Place it on an old newspaper and cover your picture with black paint. Watch what happens to your fireworks.

▷ In Thailand, villagers hold a festival called Bun Bang Fai, to make sure the rains come. They light enormous rockets.

◁ The Kabuki theatre, in Japan, began over 300 years ago. All the parts were played by men. Many Kabuki plays are still performed in Japan today.

△ The Japanese tea ceremony teaches that even everyday actions should be thought about deeply.

481

Australasia and the Pacific Islands

Australasia's largest countries are Australia, Papua New Guinea and New Zealand. In the Pacific Ocean there are thousands of islands that we call the Pacific Islands. Some are too tiny to see on a map. Over this enormous area, there are hot deserts, cold mountains and warm tropical seas.

△ Australasia and the Pacific Islands cover the enormous red area shown above.

▷ The Sydney Opera House, Australia, is a very famous landmark. It was built to look like sailing boats in the harbour. The bridge behind it links north and south Sydney, the largest city in Australia.

▽ Wellington is the capital of New Zealand. The city is famous for its steep hills and its very strong winds.

Word box
National Parks are large, protected areas where wildlife can live in safety.
Reefs are ridges of coral that build up below the surface of the sea.
Aborigines are people who lived in Australia long before Europeans arrived.

◁ Fjordland is a National Park along the southwest coast of New Zealand. It is a protected area, so people are not allowed to build on it. It is known for its beautiful mountains and scenery.

▷ The Great Barrier Reef, off the Australian coast, is the largest coral reef in the world. Thousands of tourists visit the colourful coral reef each year.

▽ Uluru, or Ayers Rock, is sacred to the Australian Aborigines. Its caves are covered with ancient paintings.

▷ These giant stone statues are on Easter Island in Polynesia. No one knows who carved them. Traditional stories tell of the statues walking to their resting place, helped by a magical power.

Farming and industry

The farm and factory products from Australasia and the Pacific Islands are very popular in other countries. Japan is one of the main buyers of goods from Australia, New Zealand and Papua New Guinea.

New Zealand has more sheep than people. The sheep are sold worldwide.

△ Sheep shearers in New Zealand often travel from farm to farm. Some can shear a sheep in under a minute!

△ Australian sheep farms are so large that farmers use planes and trucks to get around them. At shearing time, sheep are driven into sheds to have their wool cut off.

◁ Sugar is the island of Fiji's most important crop. Many people earn their living by working on sugar plantations.

▷One of the world's largest copper mines is on the island of Bougainville, Papua New Guinea. Apart from the pure copper sold, small amounts of gold also come from this mine.

Find the answers

What is an opal?

What is Fiji's most important crop?

△South Australia grows lots of grapes that are used for making wine. It is so popular that many thousands of litres are sold at home and abroad every year.

△Almost all the world's opals come from Australia. Opals are milky-coloured gemstones with other threads of colour in them. They are used in jewellery, such as rings and bracelets.

485

Australian traditions

The first people settled in Australia about 40,000 years ago. These people were called Aborigines. Although many Aboriginal people now live in cities, there are a number who live in the outback, or areas of wilderness. These people have followed their own traditions for thousands of years.

Many Australians came from Europe and Asia and still follow the traditions of their original countries.

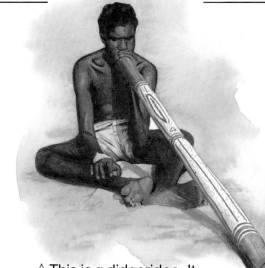

△ This is a didgeridoo. It is a musical instrument which makes a long, droning sound, like a loud bee. Didgeridoos play the background sound to many Aborigine songs.

Make a rock painting

Stuff a large, strong paper bag with

newspaper and seal top edges with sticky tape. Paste glue over the front. Cover with sand. Leave to dry. Draw simple stick figures and animals with wax crayons on sandy side.

△ Paintings and carvings created thousands of years ago, can be seen on rocks and in caves today. Many of them tell old Aborigine stories.

▷Aborigines have used boomerangs for hunting and sport for thousands of years. If thrown properly, they come right back to the thrower.

◁This camel race is part of a big sports day. Watching and taking part in sports competitions is an important part of Australian life.

▷Australians enjoy outdoor life. On a sunny day, people often put on sunscreen cream and go to the seaside. Surfing is a favourite sport.

Island traditions

Early Polynesians were adventurous sailors. They braved the unknown seas in small, light boats, searching for new lands. Finally, they settled on many of the Pacific Islands.

Traditions were handed down from family to family and are still part of everyday life today.

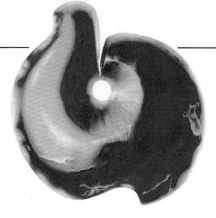

△ Amulets, or lucky pendants, have been worn by Maori people for hundreds of years. This one is worn, or placed in the water while fishing, to help the owner catch many fish.

◁ In Papua New Guinea, men hold meetings and ceremonies in spirit houses called Haus Tambarans. These have life-size wooden figures, or spirits, that watch over the village.

▷ Hawaiian dancing is called hula. Hula dancers have special costumes and often wear garlands around their necks. Stories are chanted while the dancing takes place.

Index

This index will help you to find out where you can read information about a subject. It is in alphabetical order. Each section is under a large letter of the alphabet. A main entry and its page numbers are printed in **dark**, or **bold**, letters. This is where you will find the most information. Below a main entry, there may be a second list. This shows other places in the book where you can find further information on your subject.